WITHDRAWN

Thy Love is Better than Wine

Raymond S. Nelson

Art Work by Stan Nelson

1994

Thy Love Is Better Than Wine
© 1994 by Raymond S. Nelson

First Edition
Printed in the United States of America

The title of the book is taken from the Song of Solomon 1:2

The cover photograph taken by Raymond S. Nelson.

Printed by Multi Business Press, Hillsboro, Kansas

Publishers Cataloging in Publication
(Prepared by Quality Books Inc.)

Nelson, Raymond S.
    Thy love is better than wine / Raymond S. Nelson
    p. cm.
    Preassigned LCCN: 93-81210.
    ISBN 1-882420-11-X

    I. Title

PS3564.E4746T4 1994   811'.54
                                  QBI94-225

FOREWORD

A sonnet is a little song. It is word music expressed in a set form, a form that has been used for centuries. Most people know that Shakespeare wrote sonnets. So did John Milton and William Wordsworth, among other notables. It is a resilient form, very receptive to contemporary thoughts and feelings.

Most readers associate sonnets with love, properly so. But Milton, Wordsworth, and Gerard Hopkins wrote memorable sonnets on religious and philosophical themes almost exclusively. Within these pages I explore many themes and ideas in an effort to tell the truth about love and life within the discipline of a classic form.

A traditional sonnet is a fourteen line poem, each line containing ten syllables. And there are two common rhyme schemes, the one called Italian (Petrarchan) and the other English (Shakespearean). There is also a logical structure to each of the forms.

Both forms exist in this collection of sonnets, although I have not hesitated to distort the form slightly in rhyme or rhythm (even length) if the poem demanded such modification. The important thing, ultimately, is that the poem please the reader while at the same time offering him or her some insight or scene or experience or emotion.

All of the sonnets in this collection embody several characteristics of my poetry. I use everyday words whenever possible, most of them one and two syllables. I use normal word order, and I write about common human experiences. You should find yourself and your friends on almost every page. Enjoy.

TABLE OF CONTENTS

ILLUSTRATIONS

CREDITS

"Peerless," "Heaven and Hell," "Mantrap" renamed "Anticipation," "Family Treasures," "Constancy," and "When I Consider" appeared formerly in my *Reflections on Life*, Winston-Derek Publisher, Nashville, Tennessee, 1987.

"Respite," "Kerstin," "Maytime," "Quintessence," "Till I Met You," "Infinite Variety," and "My Love" appeared formerly in my *Tracings*, The Atelier Press, Columbia, Maryland, 1989.

Dedication

To Margaret

The pearl of greatest price is she
The gem of highest worth,
The diadem which crowns my life
And beautifies the earth.

BEHOLD THIS LIVING STONE

Robert Herrick

1

SONNET

A sonnet is a timeless monument,
Fit tribute to the lasting joy that marks
Our precious memories, rich and redolent
Of rare companionship and youthful larks.
    It celebrates accumulated years
    From birth of love to rich maturity,
    Compendium of pleasure, pain, and fears,
    Distilling essence of our odyssey.
It mirrors all the days we've spent as one
While raising children, tending Mom and Dad,
Maintaining home while daily work was done
Until our days found little more to add.
    A sonnet freezes time that runs apace
    Compressing thought and passion in short space.

DAY LILIES

Each lovely lily lasts just for a day.
Its evanescent beauty fades too fast,
For essence of perfection cannot stay.
Glories soon decay; they never last.
    Incomparable blossoms! Some are shy
    And dainty, others gaudy, even bold.
    Gentle pastels, violent colors vie
    For notice from their garden bed freehold.
Hybrids are the prizes, but the ones
That Grandma knew are the homespun kind
Which massed like yellow moons or orange suns
Behind the fence or where the myrtle vined.
The wealth of worlds exists in just one bloom
And adds rare opulence to any room.

Day Lilies

CINDER

Cinder was a dog of nameless breed,
A ball of fluffy fur just footstool high.
    Her saucy, sassy tail declared her need
    To speak her mind and bargain with her eye.
    If mastiffs neared, she voiced antipathy,
    And squirrels put her in a dither. Games
        Were fun, she thought, and played them endlessly.
        To watch and supervise were her clear aims.
        She loved her family and watched the door
        Should strangers come that way. If left alone,
            She mourned and pined and would not eat. Her core
            Of being was the ones who shared her home.
            Great of heart, she earned the special place
            Accorded her by those who shared her space.

FROM OUR KITCHEN WINDOW

They come in crowds all winter to the feeders
In our yard—finches, redbirds, jays,
Sparrows, juncoes, blackbirds—all are heeders
Of the dangers as they flit and fly away.
They keep a weather eye for hawks and cats
While feeding on the grain, and small birds jump
When large ones come to dominate the flats
Arranged and filled to keep our winged friends plump.
    We hear them through our window, chattering
    Away, dispersing them in clouds by noise
    We make within from dishes clattering
    In the sink. In moments they regain their poise,
    Returning to the board; each day we care,
    Each day they share, a comfortable affair.

LOVE AFFAIR

John's lifelong love affair was with the land.
He early walked behind a plow, his horse
A choice companion, testing with his hand
The fertile soil, then following in course
With harrow, disc, and drill. He sowed the seed
And cultivated corn and beans and wheat
Until, by fall, he filled his bins to feed
Himself and hundreds more. Then, to compete,
He bought a tractor and combine, but kept
His faith with seasons, crops, with sun and rain,
Until at eighty years he grudging stepped
Aside to younger limbs. He made it plain
To all that living close to seed and soil
These many years had recompensed his toil.

LOVE IS BEST

Robert Browning

ANTICIPATION

Jo circled slowly round the laden board
To verify that all things were in place.
She turned her full attention to the lace
And crystal, silverware and plate, but scored
Her triumph in the rosebud blooms which soared
Above the goblets' fragile, slender grace
In unifying strength. The dining space,
She seemed to say, was ready to afford
Him welcome.
  One quick last glance she threw
  Before she set the stereo music low
  And lit the twelve-inch tapers, with a view
  To being ready when he came, to show
  Him warm attentive care in hopes he too
  Might find her what he had in mind to know.

YOUNG MAN'S VISION

Remember, Dear, that summer day when first
We met? In summer camp, where hundreds met
And mixed, where faces blurred en masse? How yet
I saw one single face and form that burst
On me like vintage to a man athirst?
How, then, we laughed and walked and talked to get
To know each other in that press? I'll bet
My eyes were starry when the crowd dispersed.
     I carried with me visions of a girl
     Who filled my dreams. I fixed your image deep
     Within my soul, a shrine where still you stand.
     I knew that from a myriad host one pearl
     Of greatest price I'd found; and now I'll keep
     That priceless treasure safe till life shall end.

TILL I MET YOU

From adolescent dreams of phantom girls
Or houris dancing in my head, in form
As graceful as gazelles in flight through swirls
Of grass, or swallow swept before a storm;
    From ancient scenes of damsels in my mind,
    Quite often wraiths of fiction from a page,
    Came nagging worries I might miss the kind
    Of maid I longed for when I came of age;
From medieval maidens pure as snow
And visions of chaste ladies none might kiss
Came anxious thoughts that I might never know
The pleasures of pure love and nuptial bliss;
    Till I met you and found in perfect mesh
    A blend of mystery with solid flesh.

This Perfect Place

MY MARY

I've waited till this perfect place and time,
My Mary, to ask you to become my wife.
    The waterfall, the song of birds, the chime
    Of faroff bells, the scent of spring, all rife
    With life and freshness, blend to help me say
    How much I love you. Dreams now spur me on.
    Your lovely face and form enrich each day
    For me, but I focus even more upon
    Your gracious spirit and your friendly ways.
        I offer you my faith and constancy,
        And pledge to share in honor all my days.
        If, by saying yes, you'll favor me,
        Our marriage will assure us such deep joy
        That nothing from without can it destroy.

WEDDING SONG

I watched her coming down the aisle to me,
Radiant in her white lace wedding gown,
A vestal virgin in her purity
And graceful movement from her toe to crown.
We met, and hand in hand, approached the priest
Who waited at the altar for our vows.
    "Wilt have this woman?..." and before he ceased
    His query, I replied, "I do." His brows
    Relaxed into a smile, then said to her,
    "Wilt have this man?..." when she with dignity
    Replied, "I will." The rest is but a blur
        Of faces, greetings, hugs, till we were free
        That night in May to share the nuptial bed
        In custom ours, by right, since we were wed.

ONE ON ONE

When wedding bonds are lightly borne, and each
Lives for the other, sacred monuments
To faith are built as both aspire to reach
The ultimate in life. The consequence
Of honored love in dalliance or duty
Is mutual fulfillment. Each creates
The other. Borglum's classic lines of beauty
Lack in worth what each achieves in states
Of being.
       Chisels, hammers for the soul
    Are trust and truth and care and kindness. These,
    With patience, skill, and vision for the whole,
    Assure a pair as rare as a Doric frieze.
       Living art takes nurture, grace, and time,
       Epitome of craftsmanship sublime.

The Sound of Music

MARGARET

My life with you is like a symphony.
Our busy days fill each melodic line
With contrapuntal magic, certain sign
We satisfy the laws of harmony.
Your low pitched treble voice blends easily
In stirring choral passages with mine,
A baritone, as we each day combine
Our lives in major and in minor key.
The pace moves from allegro to a smooth
Andante, graceful largo, or a beat
As quick as scherzo, presto, menuet
Con brio, while ever-shifting rhythms soothe
Or grate from hour to hour in the heat
Of sharing daily life in our duet.

MY DEAR

My life with you is like a symphony
Where melody and rhythm interface
With harmony and timbre to embrace
The range of sounds available to me.
Composers often use a minor key
To set the tone by which the notes can race
Or plod, as joy and sorrow interlace
In music to create a unity.
Our lives entwine in spirit and in flesh
As each creates the other every day.
Life's plagues and wants we sturdily survive
—its storms and floods and drouths—as we enmesh
Our love and care and strength that we might say
In harmony: together we're alive!

THE GREATEST GOOD

Robert Browning

PEERLESS

Every rose is special, no two are
The same. Petals curl in petals, till blooms
Are fully blown, and fragrant mists float far
Afield to fuse with other spring perfumes.
    Each oak tree is different, each one stands
    Alone, reaching broadly, reaching tall,
    With no two crowns alike. For each commands
    Its proper due and place in midst of all.
A man's beloved is peerless, shares her place
With none. Her form, her grace, her poise, her charm
Combine through matchless means to make her face
The symbol of perfection naught can harm.
    Each rose and oak and woman is unique,
    My dear; you are the treasure that I seek.

MAYTIME

The rains of May bejewel the graceful blooms
That flourish in the fields and garden plots,
Mute symbols of the fruit of nests and wombs
The wanton season from its store allots,
While Sol peers out in turn to lure all life
To graceful form as vital force combines
With humble dust to shape a world as rife
With creatures as the stars that nightly shine.
    The planet throbs with teeming life, as one
    By one each creature pairs in Nature's way
    Fulfilling purposes beyond the ken
    Of man despite the urgent powers at play.
        In such a world I sought a loving mate
        And, finding you, exist in favored state.

CONSTANCY

The old-time products, ways of doing things,
Are gone. All things become "improved" or "new,"
And force time-honored ways to take to wings
As upstart ways replace the tried and true.
    Nothing's free from change. Our house, once bare,
    Now nestles deep within the shrubs and trees
    We set as saplings, watered, trimmed with care,
    Until our acre should by blooming please.
Our friends, who watched them grow, have through the years
Begun to age and wither, some to fail,
And some to go, till I am left with fears
We too shall weaken, battered by time's flail.
    Yet in this steady flux I find you true;
    I celebrate the constancy I find in you.

A Clamorous World

RESPITE

The headlines in the papers rage and scream
Of murder, theft, extortion, rape, and war;
The newscasts join their noise by adding more
On hate, intrigue, deception, plot, and scheme
Until I feel submerged in waves that seem
To threaten life itself. The constant roar
Of men and nations locked in combat for
Low ends destroys most hope for mankind's dream.
    Yet in such heavy seas I find a beach,
    A haven from the violent storms that beat
    The world. I find in you a loving wife,
    A place of quiet peace and joy, where speech
    Or silence is serene, where I retreat
    Each day to your embrace from endless strife.

BOWER OF BLISS

We moved from "overdrive" and "dynaflow"
One day to "microwaves" and "microchips"
The next, plus "lunar flights" and "astral trips"
Computed in detail to "all things go."
With superconductivity in tow,
Genetic engineering well in place,
Our technocrats now seek to lead the race
To destinies beyond our ken to know.
I hear their spokesmen, read their scripts, then turn
From them to dear redemptive things: your smiles,
Your loving words, your warm embrace, your kiss.
I leave that complex outer world, I yearn
For simple things. You are my rest from trials
That plague the daily scene. You are my bliss.

KERSTIN

I watched the teeming masses in the Mall
(the quick and slow, the tall and short, each hue
And race, some fat some thin, some large some small)
And wondered how I chanced to merit you.
I studied people, weighed each sight and sound—
I heard shrill voices, dulcet tones, the tread
Of feet on pavement, squealing children bound
For fun while parents followed where they led.
I pondered all the shapes and sizes, all
The millions on this earth, thought how each
Is special, yet how each one can enthrall
A lover, doting sweetheart, through sweet speech.
I marvel how from all that myriad crew
I am so blessed as to share my life with you.

QUINTESSENCE

An ancient singer sang of breasts like roes,
Of navel, neck, and lips, and young love's day;
I sing in echo, flesh with soul compose,
And revel in our love through life's long way.
The world's cosmetic pow'rs attempt in vain
To match the radiance of your eyes, your skin,
Your silver hair, the smile you never feign:
All witness to the peace that reigns within.
The beauty of your body blends with soul
As graceful form affirms your spirit's health,
And quiet poise attests a living whole
In keeping with substantial inner wealth.
The real and superficial stand quite clear:
In you are goodness, strength, and love sincere.

HEAVEN OR HELL

I know where heaven is. It's in your smile,
Your loving presence, all you do and say.
It's in the hours we spend at work and play,
The gentle words which lack pretense and guile.
It's walking hand in hand each patient mile
Or standing side by side at household chore.
It's sharing joy and sorrow, less and more,
In faith and hope that make each day worthwhile.
I know of hell as well. It's in the void,
The echoes sounding through each empty room
Where otherwise your cheery voice would sound
With mine. It's in long tedious hours employed,
Then weary evenings, silent as a tomb.
It's missing you as earth spins round and round.

WHEN I CONSIDER...

When I consider how my days are spent
In philosophic quest on spongy soil
Or futile sessions mired in precedent,
In jangling strife or ministrative toil;
    When I encounter greedy, grasping men
    Who mask their avaricious ways in guile,
    Or selfish souls whose only regimen
    Consists of egocentric ploy or wile;
When I have jounced and bounced on bumpy streets,
And threaded carefully through crowded halls
Beneath an incubus of noise that beats
And throbs until I reach my office walls;
I draw a breath, relax, and think of you,
Restored thereby to face the day anew.

LET ME COUNT THE WAYS

Elizabeth Barrett Browning

MY LOVE

I've watched your life unfold these many years
And thought how like the blowing of a rose—
A precious bud in infancy appears
In early prints, then in each Christmas pose.
    I've watched each petal open, curling free,
    As I found grace in wedlock by your side
    And saw each child grow up, as meant to be,
    Where love and trust securely could abide.
Since when, the blossom's radiated joy
In daily service, time in prayer, in strength
That grew despite the blights that might destroy.
I know, of course, all growth must cease at length.
    The petals soon must wilt, must dry, must fall—
    Unless God choose to press the bloom, and call.

FAMILY TREASURES

I like the feel of old but precious things. . .
The kitchen table which the children scarred,
The walnut chest restored though somewhat marred,
The old oak rockers where we sit like kings
To view our wedding plate while my soul sings,
The antique bedroom set we share at rest,
The ancient cherry chair. . . these all attest
To ease of life. Each quiet comfort brings.
    I like to hold your hand, to view your face,
    To reminisce in fondness, touch your hair,
    To talk or show my love through an embrace
    That says (I hope) you are to me most fair.
    How fitting, then, while we grow old apace
    We have the old familiar things to share.

Family Hearth

INFINITE VARIETY

I thought of course you'd nothing new to show.
From twenty years of wedded life I knew
(I thought) I had you figured out. I know
How false that is from what I've seen ensue.
I felt a quiet stubbornness when you
Began on principle last year to go
To class to learn of Shakespeare and pursue
New skills. You were determined then to grow.
The Serpent of Old Nile beguiled her man
With infinite variety in deed
And word. He marveled at her grace
And loved her at the end as he began.
Like Antony of old, I'll never cede
My claim; surprise me till I've run my race!

CEREMONY OF INNOCENCE

Silver wedding bells ring out their chimes
To register the years you two have shared
Your lives. You've laughed together many times,
And wept a few. You've shouldered burdens, cared
For duties, filled your roles, until today
We honor you. Your children are the hallmark
Of a home where love and friendship reign. They play
The game of life with spirit, task or lark
The same. You now must write new chapters, fill
Each page of daily life with tales drawn new
From classroom, farmstead, merchant, shop, until
You rest your pen, in years remote from view.
You've only just begun, you know, to tell
Your whole life's story. But you've started well.

ANNIVERSARY

I've shared your bed for forty years; we've bred
The fruit of love. My body long has shown
The scars, the wrinkles, spots and hoary head
Which witness to the years now long since flown.
Yet patiently you hold my hand. . . you've known
My worst and best; each day you nurture me
Through love that has in forty years so grown
That other precious pearl I cannot see.
What then if stiffening limbs encumber us,
Or eyes and ears grow dim? What then if breath
Grow short, or body shrink? We will not fuss
But live each day as lovers do till death
Part us forever. Come, come, my dear. I'll hold
You in my heart till my last days are told.

APPLY THINE HEART TO UNDERSTANDING

Solomon

THE DREAM

We lift our eyes to Venus in the east
And dream of endless triumphs in the quest
For fame and fortune. Long before the feast
Can be enjoyed, we struggle with each test
Of skill and fortitude and iron will.
    To be a Black Belt, or to play like Liszt,
    To spin a yarn like Hemingway, or fill
    The walls with sketches, represent a list
    Of high achievements not beyond our grasp
    To seek perfection.
                There the dream, right now
    The discipline. We work today to clasp
    The prize tomorrow. Crowns may grace our brow
    If we with single mind pursue the goal
    That will inscribe our name on honor's roll.

WORK

"If they will not work, they shall not eat,"
The prophet said. "All persons pull their weight
In best societies and seek to meet
The daily round as masters of their fate."
Much more, their work defines the very being
They become. Each artist, clerk, or priest
Is largely formed by skills achieved in seeing
Duties done—the same for great and least.
    Work is not a curse, and never was.
    Positions call for creativity
    And bring fulfillment, vision, strength, and cause
    To serve which otherwise might never be.
    Work with hands or head or heart or all
    Produces harvests rich beyond recall.

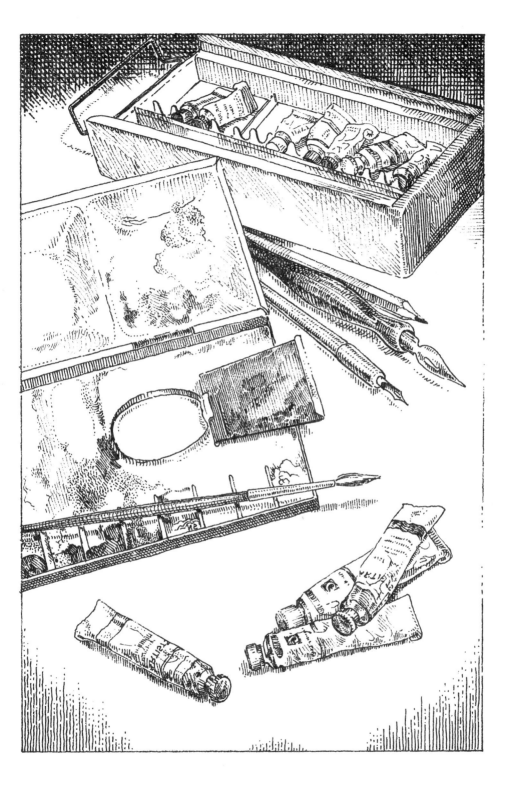

The Craftsman's Tools

LIFE

The falcon stoops to snatch a vixen's cubs
As she exists on rabbits, chicks, or mice.
Such prey survive on roots or grains or grubs
Until the wheel of chance exacts the price
Of life from them in turn. The chains of life
Enfetter plant and animal alike—
There is no escape. The deadly strife
Continues as all earthly species strike
Or are themselves the struck. Not even man
Avoids the cycles, eating Nature's pledge
To days to come: each egg, each fruit, each grain
Contains the promise of a future, edge
Of destiny aborted or attained.
Life is always struggle, nothing sure,
A promise and a challenge to endure.

UNITY

The universe attends me every day.
I embrace the stars a million miles
Away as readily as grass or files
Of dew-drenched summer blooms or new-mown hay,
Embrace the trees that line each right of way
To fashion airy temples with long aisles
Alive with birds and insects, wooded isles
Of sheer delight where light and shadows play.
    The infinite and finite blend as one
    To make my daily life pure mystery.
    I marvel as I watch clear drops of dew
    Transformed to prisms in the morning sun
    And think that Nature's face can sometimes be
    Unveiled to bring some inner truth to view.

DAZZLING DARKNESS

I saw the other side of light last night
And puzzled why all things stretch out from pole
To pole—the yin and yang, the flesh and soul,
The good and ill, the live and dead, great might
And frailty, true and false, jet black and white—
Vast aggregates of poles which form the whole
Wherein we function and fulfill the role
Assigned at birth, a disconcerting plight.
     I look within, as Dante did, and find
     A host of opposites and have to choose
     The right or wrong—a child of earth inclined
     To good or evil in the fight to lose
     Or win the daily round, an eidolon
     Of God, with hopes and dreams to lead me on.

FAMILY

Blood and marriage weave the web which ties
Our lives together. Parents interlace
Genetic strands to form complex allies
And companies in life's e'erchanging face.
From brothers, sisters, cousins, uncles, aunts,
    To stepsons, in-laws, foster kin, and more,
    Come clans who supervise mankind's advance
    To rich relationships secure in lore
    Derived from centuries of nurturing
    The human enterprise. Old childhood feuds
    Long gone, or differing views, now merely bring
    A piquancy to shifting family moods.
When they know all, and love you anyway,
You are a family. Let come what may.

MOTHER

Is mother home? Home to tend the kids
And manage family affairs? She
Kisses hurts away and fondly bids
Her little ones to solace at her knee.
A mother is the keystone of the arch
Or (change the figure) center of the sphere
In any settled home. She steals a march
On all disruption if it should appear.
Her children rise to call her blessed though
It may take years before they know how much
She sacrificed for them and what they owe
To her. A mother gives and gives, soft touch
In matters of the heart to near and dear,
To reap rewards in love that grow each year.

MEMORIES

Memories make the present come alive.
Cooking Sunday dinners makes me think
Of Mother and her roasts, and when I drive
To Grandpa's farm, the sounds and settings link
Today with Christmas celebrations, songs
And stories, cows and chickens, horse and plow,
Retrieved from long ago. The past belongs
    To daily intercourse, and then and now
    Fuse deep within. My job, I must confess,
    Rests clearly on the skills I learned ten years
    Or more ago, and habits I possess
    Began when roaming childhood's busy spheres.
All that I think and do and am today
Depends on thoughts and acts of yesterday.

READY FOR BED

The children jumped and bounced all over John,
Dressed in nighties, giggling as they pushed
His paper down. He had a C D on,
And half an eye on news before they rushed
To smother him with tiny bodies, shouts
Of laughter, streaming hair, and drumming fists.
John set all aside, for nightly bouts
Like this were ritual and headed lists
Of family lore and life. I watched the scene
Until the two were bundled off to bed,
Then listened as he said, "Each day I mean
To let them tussle. It won't last. Instead
They'll soon be ladies, a prim and proper pair.
I'll just have my music, news, and chair."

CALL ME MARA

Naomi

BECOMING ONE

When tempers rise and bitter words ensue
From him who means the world to you—forgive.
When he is always late, for all you do,
Be philosophic and—forgive. To live
Together happily demands a wise
Maturity. Should he forget your day—
Your special day—be patient, but apprise
Him of his fault. And if, by chance, he play
The fool and break his wedding vow, then come
To you repentant, with a mind to pray
Forgiveness, do be gracious. Don't succumb
To thoughts of vengeance or despair. The way
To healing lies through truth and trust, and growth
To oneness, day by day, rests with you both.

The Chill of Winter

LETTING GO

"Dad, I can do it on my own"
Rang in my ears long after we had talked.
My little girl, now twenty, seemed to phone
Less often—worse, she almost always balked
At counsel that I tried to give. I know
She's grown, but can't forget the wreck she had
And how she needed me. I want to show
Her where the hazards are. I'd be so glad
To save her heartaches. She's so young and still
So trusting. I remember how they teased
Her for her awkwardness and braces till
I found her home in tears. Well, I've displeased
Her quite enough. She needs a larger yard
To play in, so I'll let her, though it's hard.

TOO LATE

"I wish I'd told her just how much I cared,"
He said to me with reddened eyes, his voice
Stretched thin from deep emotion. "I haven't shared
With her for years. It was my wilful choice,
And now she's gone." I knew the family
And how the son had gone his way despite
A loving mother's heart. No human plea,
No earthly referee could make things right.
      I thought of all the ones who pass that way,
      Who fail to share with loved ones when they can
      And learn too late that care expressed today
      Is never wasted, never lost. Our span
      Of years invites the best that life affords:
      To love and be beloved, expressed in words.

SIMONE

So many kids grow up too soon today.
I'm thinking of Simone. She had a child
Just yesterday at age fifteen. They say
Her parents kicked her out as being wild.
She's raised herself. No one's been at home
For years to care for her. Her grades are poor,
And chances are she'll fail at school. She'll roam
From place to place and job to job, obscure
And soon forgotten by her peers. She may,
Like others, go the welfare route, or turn
To other men and complicate her way
By breeding more. If only she could learn
Self-discipline, complete her education,
Turn herself around, and grasp…tradition.

SUSAN

Her face looked old beyond her years. Inured
To being mother's helper in the home,
She bore her lot with patience. She endured
The chores a growing family brought, her own
Sweet will long hostage to imperious needs
Of others. Laundry, cleaning, cooking, childcare
Filled her hours after school. The seeds
Of mutiny lay long since dead. Aware
How much her parents' love embraced the brood,
She did her part full willingly. The price
She paid, the truth to say, was somber mood
And loss of childhood's carefree ways. The spice
Of life has little lure for her, and may
Elude her grasp until her dying day.

HOME ALONE

With Amos gone, my life seems inside out,
The seams exposed, the pattern all awry.
My days at work are not so bad, no doubt
Because I'm busy. Evenings I apply
Myself to eating, sewing, reading, just
To fill the hours until I go to bed—
Alone. I miss his touch, his wit, but must
Press on in spite of emptiness ahead.
    I have the kids, of course, and speak each week
    With them (or write) and friends (though mostly pairs).
    They wish me well, yet even as I speak
    I sense the gulf which yawns despite their care.
I wonder if I'll ever turn things right-
Side-out again. I do not know tonight.

Clouded Skies

CLOUDED SKIES

A pall hangs low above the city now
Where thousands of our best are out of work.
Dark memories of soup lines shade the brow
Of those who saw the thirties and each quirk
Of fate—like brokers selling apples on
The street. Worried couples watch the first
Approaching, bills already high upon
The spindle, savings gone. They fear the worst—
Loss of home, of car; their children's needs.
They bend beneath the load of mutual stress,
Tempers short and speeches curt. Frail reeds,
They sometimes break, and sometimes stand the press.
In times like these, strength comes from deep within,
Divinely led to face the worst and win.

WHEN LOVE GOES

When love goes, what is left? The dreams of youth
Lie ashes on the grate, you say, or worse,
Are cauldrons filled with hate and spite and curse
Upon the head of former mate, with truth
A weapon meant to hurt. The law's sharp tooth
Too often tears the flesh once dear, with purse
And offspring prize, each willing to coerce
The other. Hate leaves little room for ruth.
    When love goes, mansions lie in ruin and waste.
    Children's wounded psyches needing care
    Cry out in pain. And former lovers based
    In separate camps spue venom. Friends despair,
    For partners can no longer be embraced
    As one; they scorn to function as a pair.

THE SILENT SUMMONS

"It's traveled to the liver as I feared,"
She said. My eighty-year-old neighbor spoke
In steady, vibrant tones as I peered
Into her lined, unclouded face. I broke
The silence which ensued with "Are they sure?"
I'd known about the cancer in her eye
But waited for more tests in hope a cure
Might still be found. "Oh, yes. And I won't try
To outwit fate. I'm going on that trip
To Rome with Vincent. Then let come what may."
I'd known her quiet courage and her grip
On passion many years. What could I say?
I marveled at the grace with which she faced
The silent summons as the seconds raced.

MISTAKE

When aged George laid Edith to her rest,
He lived a widower two years, or three,
Then met a seeming paragon. He guessed
She'd fill the void that Edith left and free
His life from loneliness. They wed. And Hyde
Emerged from Jekyll overnight. She kept
Him from his friends and church. She daily tried
To change his ways—even where he slept!
Mild-mannered George was sore perplexed. He would
Not seek divorce. The paragon-turned-shrike
Laid siege to every single thing she could
Until her man gave up. He would not strike
Nor do her ill. Withdrawn, confused, austere,
A broken man, he died within the year.

HAIL AND FAREWELL

Alfred Lord Tennyson

LOVE REBLOOMED

Ruth, near eighty, lived on a Flint Hills farm
Alone. Pretty, with a tipped-up nose
And sparkling eye, she had the power to charm
Her friends and neighbors. From her many beaus
In youth she'd chosen one and lived with him
In love until he died. When Chester learned
Of Ruth's sore loss, he paused an interim
Before he called his childhood friend. She turned
A friendly ear to him because she knew
He'd lost his mate some years before. She chose
To let him pay her court because the two
Knew well it is not good or right to close
The gates on life too soon. The bonnie pair
Then wed, delighting friends from everywhere.

PERSPECTIVE

The years have flown like birds across the sky,
Poised on graceful wing, soon lost to view.
The vast expanse that spread before my eye
In youth has strangely shrunk as I pursue
My vagrant memories. Young Time once crept
From day to day, and dreams seemed not to end,
But looking back from age my vistas kept
Contracting; everything came near at hand:
    It wasn't long ago I'd schooled, then wed,
    Then seen my children born. I still can see
    My first slow steps at work, which slowly sped
    Until retirement last year now sets me free.
        I see my life with different eyes in age
        Than I could ever hope in youth to gauge.

Prairie Vista

TILL DEATH US DO PART

When George and Edith finished forty years
Of married life, she had a stroke that left
Her helpless. He became her nurse. His ears
And eyes and hands and feet were hers, all deft
In ministration. Morning, noon, and night
He met her needs. He washed and dressed and fed
His charge. He brushed her hair, he took delight
In taking her by wheelchair from her bed
To friends at home or church. Her mind was clear
And, though she could not speak or write with ease,
She tried to keep in touch with longtime peers.
The road was rough, and days were long, and keys
To happiness were sometimes lost. But then
They shook themselves, looked up, and tried again.

FINAL EXIT

I searched her delicately moulded face
For signs of weakness and found none. She bore
The weight of final illness with a grace
That chastened me. On pallid lips she wore
A smile belied by pain and fevered brow,
Which long had been her lot. Her form
Was slight, wasted in the struggle, now
Mere whisper of her strength before the storm
Of illness laid her low. Her eyes were bright—
Unnaturally bright—as spirit fought
With flesh, and won. Indomitable sprite!
At peace with God, with self, with all, she sought
The elemental stuff of life each day
And let the fluff and flotsam float away.

SHIFT OF SCENE

When Wang Sechang surveyed his war-torn land,
A place where stores were empty, croplands bare,
Where power lines were idle, ventures banned,
With grief and gloom suspended in the air,
He came to Kansas and began again.

He found shelves groaning from around the earth,
The wheat fields lush, and cattle fat in pens.
He marveled at the fashions, things of worth
In entertainment—music, films, and books—
And appliances which served a hundred ways.
He traveled freely, happy with the looks
Of plenty at each turn. He spent his days
　　　Rebuilding life, while feeling like a king
　　　Surrounded by supplies of...everything.

TIME AND CHANCE

Ecclesiastes

PEACE

I draw a breath of early morning air
In cool of summer or in winter's chill
And revel in the rain or sun, aware
Of wonders that each moment may distill.
I have learned to taste a raisin and
To value water's worth; I prize the rich
Patina on my antique flower stand
And finger Grandma's afghan, where each stitch
Came from her hand. I focus on the sounds—
The glorious sounds—as music fills the room,
Then pause to sense the fragrance that abounds
From fresh-cut garden flowers in full bloom.
Such priceless treasures fill my life each day
And bring me peace that little can allay.

LIGHTBEARER

Afraid to alter speech or dress or deed,
The many march in lockstep day by day
In docile bondage to broad social sway
As yokes secure them to their long held creed.
A mirror rules the ones who others heed
Too much, as norms determine what they say,
And cause the mass, like sheep, to make their way
In herds who know to follow not to lead.

But you, my friend, are like a lamp alight
Concerned not only with what others do
But free to seek fresh paths within the night
Of dreary custom, shining like those few
Who press through this dark vale with undimmed sight
To win long cherished goals. I honor you.

HOPE RESTORED

When Glen and Toby went their separate ways
Because of seven troubled years, she thought
She'd never love again. She needed space.
Mistrusting men, she walked alone. She taught
Herself to solo, wouldn't play the field
Lest she be hurt once more. In church one day
A cleareyed man slipped next to her, appealed
To share her songbook. Unsure what to say,
She almost ran. He gently paid her court,
Till after months she slowly found her voice
Enough to say, "I love you, Dan." In short,
She found new verve and life, and could rejoice
In confidence renewed. She learned that care
And kindness are the bonds true lovers wear.

The Good Earth

KANSAS GOLD

When Coronado crossed the Kansas plain
In search of Seven Golden Cities, sure
He'd find Quivira and secure for Spain
Great wealth, for himself a sinecure,
He found it was a lie. He'd been misled.
  What he didn't learn is that the gold
  Was there, oil and gas within a bed
  Of rock and soil in quantities untold.
Had he lived a little longer, seen
The coming of red wheat, seen the fields
Of rippling, waving grain with their sheen
Of radiant golden ripeness and rich yields
Enough to feed the world, he would know
He had succeeded: gold above, below.

WINDMILLS

The turning blades on treeless Kansas plains
Made farms and ranches possible despite
The early judgment that elusive rains
Kept this the Great American Desert. Bright
Young settlers dug their wells and built their mills
To water herds and irrigate their crops.
Their lofty fans were landmarks on the hills
And prairies, welcome havens, welcome stops
For weary travelers on their westward trails.
The farms became oases, offering food
And water, care and shelter from the gales
That pummeled from the south. The mills, though crude
And elemental, cleared the path for days
Of growth and change that led to modern ways.

MARGUERITE

The "pearl of greatest price" takes many forms.
For some it is a sapphire blue, or gem
Of ruby hue. A diamond adorns
A favored hand or crowns a diadem.
    An emerald was Caesar's toy, while jade—
    Imperial Jade—is Burma's glory. So
    The story goes around the world. The trade
    In precious things says lots about the flow
    Of life. Some treasure gold or teak or shells,
    While others value iron, feathers, beads
    Or clay. The quest for worth and beauty tells
    It all. It matters not how one succeeds
    In showing love, concern, respect, and care.
    One simply speaks by using what is there.

NOTES

13 An *houri* is a beautiful virgin in the Koranic paradise, and *wraith* is an apparition, a ghostly figure.

17 Gutzon Borglum (1867-1941) is the sculptor who created the four figures on Mt. Rushmore in South Dakota. Doric friezes typically decorated the pediments of classical Greek public buildings.

30 The ancient singer sang "The Song of Solomon" in the Bible.

39 "Ceremony of Innocence" is an allusion to W. B. Yeats' poem, "The Second Coming."

43 Venus is the morning star.

48 The *yin* and *yang* are oriental symbols for duality.

53 *Mara* means "bitter."

66 Robert Louis Stevenson published his psychological study "The Strange Case of Dr. Jekyll and Mr. Hyde" in 1886.

74 The name *Wang* means "king" in several oriental languages.

81 Francisco Vasquez de Coronado, a Spaniard, was in 1541 the first European explorer in Kansas.

83 *Marguerite* is the French word for "pearl."

Colophon

Raymond S. Nelson, Ph. D., has taught English for thirty-eight years at two institutions, Morningside College in Sioux City, Iowa, and Friends University in Wichita. He was named Professor of English, Emeritus, in 1990, and continues to teach an occasional class at Friends. He has published five books of poetry: *Not by Bread Alone* (1982), *Reflections on Life: Birth to Death* (1987), *Tracings* (1989), *...and the Kansas Wind Blows* (1991), and *Prairie Sketches* (1992).

The artist, Stan Nelson, is Dr. Nelson's son. He is a Museum Specialist at the National Museum of American History (Smithsonian) in Washington, D.C. His specialty is type-casting, an important dimension to the history of printing.

The type face is Janson, printed on 60# Natural Nekoosa Opaque Offset paper.